THE BIBLE

See What God Made!

Genesis 1-2
(Creation)

by Mary Manz Simon

Illustrated by Dennis Jones

SPIRIT PRESS

Read and Learn the Bible
LEVEL 1

See What God Made!

Noah's Ark

David and Goliath

Jonah and the Big Fish

The Good Samaritan

Too Tall, Too Small

Jesus Blesses the Children

Fishes and Loaves

Jesus Fills the Nets

© 1990 Concordia Publishing House

This edition published in 2004 by Spirit Press, an imprint of Dalmatian Press, LLC. Used by permission. All rights reserved.

The SPIRIT PRESS name and logo are trademarks of Dalmatian Press, LLC, Franklin, Tennessee 37067.
No part of this book may be reproduced or copied in any form without the written permission of Concordia Publishing House.
ISBN: 1-40371-160-7
Printed in Canada
13771-1004

04   05   06   07   QSR   10   9   8   7   6   5   4   3   2   1

This Book Belongs to

_____
Name

_____
Date

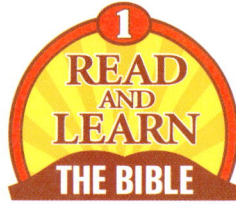

To the Adult:

Early readers need two kinds of reading. They need to be read to, and they need to do their own reading. The *Read and Learn the Bible* series helps you to encourage your child with both kinds.

For example, your child might read this book as you sit together. Listen attentively. Assist gently, if needed. Encourage, be patient, and be very positive about your child's efforts.

Then perhaps you'd like to share the selected Bible story in an easy-to-understand translation or paraphrase.

Using both types of reading gives your child a chance to develop new skills and pride in reading. You share and support your child's excitement.

As a mother and a teacher, I anticipate the joy your child will feel in saying, "Hear me read a Bible story!"

Mary Manz Simon

In the beginning God created
the heaven and the earth.
GENESIS 1:1

Look.

What will happen?

See what God made.

This is good.
This is day 1.

God made this.

This is good.
This is day 2.
What will happen next?

See what God made.

This is good.

This is day 3.

What will happen next?

Look.

God made this.

This is good.

This is day 4.

What will happen next?

See what God made.

This is good.

This is day 5.

What will happen next?

Look.
God made this.

This is good.
This is day 6.

See what God made.

This is day 7.
This is good.

This is good.

Read and Learn

13 words that tell the Bible story.

WORD LIST

is	good	this
God	look	what
see	made	will
day	make	happen
	next	

About the Author

Mary Manz Simon holds a doctoral degree in education with a specialty in early childhood education. She has taught at levels from preschool through post-graduate. Dr. Simon is the bestselling author of more than 40 children's books, including *Little Visits with Jesus*. She and her husband, the Reverend Henry A. Simon, are the parents of three children.